ESCAPE FROM REASON

Francis A. Schaeffer

Escape
from
Reason

a penetrating
analysis
of trends in
modern thought.

InterVarsity Press
Downers Grove
Illinois 60515

other books by Francis A. Schaeffer

The God Who Is There
Death in the City
Pollution and the Death of Man
The Church at the End of the 20th Century
The Mark of the Christian
He Is There and He Is Not Silent
True Spirituality
Genesis in Space and Time
Back to Freedom and Dignity
Basic Bible Studies
Art and the Bible
No Little People
Everybody Can Know (Francis & Edith Schaeffer)
Joshua and the Flow of Biblical History
How Should We Then Live?
Whatever Happened to the Human Race?

©1968 by Inter-Varsity Fellowship, England

Published in the U.S.A. by InterVarsity Press, Downers Grove, Illinois, with permission from Universities and Colleges Christian Fellowship, Leicester, England.

InterVarsity Press® is the book-publishing division of InterVarsity Christian Fellowship®, a student movement active on campus at hundreds of universities, colleges and schools of nursing in the United States of America, and a member movement of the International Fellowship of Evangelical Students. For information about local and regional activities, write Public Relations Dept., InterVarsity Christian Fellowship, 6400 Schroeder Rd., P.O. Box 7895, Madison, WI 53707-7895.

ISBN 0-87784-538-7
Library of Congress Catalog Card Number: 68-58084

Printed in the United States of America ♾

33	32	31	30	29	28	27	26	25	24
05	04	03	02	01	00	99	98		

CONTENTS

FOREWORD

If a man goes overseas for any length of time we would expect him to learn the language of the country to which he is going. More than this is needed, however, if he is really to communicate with the people among whom he is living. He must learn another language—that of the thought-forms of the people to whom he speaks. Only so will he have real communication with them and to them. So it is with the Christian church. Its responsibility is not only to hold to the basic, scriptural principles of the Christian faith, but to communicate these unchanging truths 'into' the generation in which it is living.

Every generation of Christians has this problem of learning how to speak meaningfully to its own age. It cannot be solved without an understanding of the changing existential situation which it faces. If we are to communicate the Christian faith effectively, therefore, we must know and understand the thought-forms of our own generation. These will differ slightly from place to place, and more so from nation to nation. Nevertheless there are characteristics of an age such as ours which are the same wherever we happen to be. It is these that I am especially considering in this book. And the object of this is far from being merely to satisfy intellectual curiosity. As we go along it will become clear how far-reaching are the practical consequences of a proper understanding of these movements of thought.

Some may be surprised that in analysing the trends in modern thought I should begin with Aquinas and work my way forward from there. But I am convinced that our study must be concerned at one and the same time with both history and philosophy. If we are to understand present-day trends in thought we must see how the situation has come about historically and also look in some detail at the development of philosophic thought-forms. Only when this has been done are we ready to go on to the practical aspects of how to communicate unchanging truth in a changing world.

CHAPTER ONE

Nature and grace

The origin of modern man could be traced back to
several periods. But I would begin with the teaching
of a man who changed the world in a very real way.
Thomas Aquinas (1225–1274) opened the way for the
discussion of what is usually called 'nature and grace'.
They may be set out diagrammatically like this:

GRACE

NATURE

This diagram may be amplified as follows, to show
what is included on the two different levels:

GRACE, THE HIGHER:	GOD THE CREATOR; HEAVEN AND HEAVENLY THINGS; THE UNSEEN AND ITS INFLUENCE ON THE EARTH; MAN'S SOUL; UNITY
NATURE, THE LOWER:	THE CREATED; EARTH AND EARTHLY THINGS; THE VISIBLE AND WHAT NATURE AND MAN DO ON EARTH; MAN'S BODY; DIVERSITY

Up to this time, man's thought-forms had been Byzantine. The heavenly things were all-important, and were so holy that they were not pictured realistically. For instance, Mary and Christ were never portrayed realistically. Only symbols were portrayed. So if you look up at one of the later Byzantine mosaics in the baptistry at Florence, for example, it is not a picture of Mary that you see, but a symbol representing Mary.

On the other hand, simple nature—trees and mountains—held no interest for the artist, except as part of the world to be lived in. Mountain climbing, for instance, simply had no appeal as something to be done for its own sake. As we shall see, mountain climbing as such really began with the new interest in nature. So prior to Thomas Aquinas there was an overwhelming emphasis on the heavenly things, very far off and very holy, pictured only as symbols, with little interest in nature itself. With the coming of Aquinas we have the real birth of the humanistic Renaissance.

Aquinas's view of nature and grace did not involve a complete discontinuity between the two, for he did have a concept of unity between them. From Aquinas's day on, for many years, there was a constant struggle for a unity of nature and grace and a hope that rationality would say something about both.

There were some very good things that resulted from the birth of Renaissance thought. In particular, nature received a more proper place. From a biblical viewpoint nature is important because it has been created by God, and is not to be despised. The things of the body are not to be despised when compared with the soul. The things of beauty are important. Sexual things are not evil of themselves. All these things are involved in the fact that in nature God has given us a good gift, and the man who regards them with contempt is really despising God's creation. As such he is despising, in a sense, God Himself, for he has contempt for what God has made.

Aquinas and the autonomous

At the same time, we are now able to see the significance of the diagram of nature and grace in a different way. While there were some good results from giving nature a better place, it also opened the way for much that was destructive, as we shall see. In Aquinas's view the will of man was fallen, but the intellect was not. From this incomplete view of the biblical Fall flowed all the subsequent difficulties. Man's intellect became autonomous. In one realm man was now independent, autonomous.

This sphere of the autonomous in Aquinas takes on various forms. One result, for example, was the development of natural theology. In this view, natural theology is a theology that could be pursued independently from the Scriptures. Though it was an autonomous study, he hoped for unity and said that there was a correlation between natural theology and the Scriptures. But the important point in what followed was that a really autonomous area was set up.

From the basis of this autonomous principle, philosophy also became free, and was separated from revelation. Therefore philosophy began to take wings, as it were, and fly off wherever it wished, without relationship to the Scriptures. This does not mean that this tendency was never previously apparent, but it appears in a more total way from this time on.

Nor did it remain isolated in Thomas Aquinas's philosophic-theology. Soon it began to enter the arts.

Today we have a weakness in our educational process in failing to understand the natural associations between the disciplines. We tend to study all our disciplines in unrelated parallel lines. This tends to be true in both Christian and secular education. This is one of the reasons why evangelical Christians have been taken by surprise at the tremendous shift that has come in our generation. We have studied our exegesis as exegesis, our theology as theology, our philosophy as philosophy; we study something about art as art; we study music as music, without understanding that these are things of man, and the things of man are not unrelated parallel lines.

There are several ways in which this association between theology, philosophy and the arts emerged following Aquinas.

Painters and writers

The first artist to be influenced was Cimabue (1240–1302), teacher of Giotto (1267–1337). Aquinas lived from 1225 to 1274, thus these influences were clearly felt quickly in the field of art. Instead of all the subjects of art being above the dividing line between nature and grace in the symbolic manner of the Byzantine, Cimabue and Giotto began to paint the things of nature as nature. In this transition period the change did not come all at once. Hence there was a tendency at first to paint the lesser things in the picture naturalistically, but to continue to portray Mary, for example, as a symbol.

Then Dante (1265–1321) began to write in the way that these men painted. Suddenly, everything starts to shift on the basis that nature began to be important. The same development can be seen in the writers Petrarch (1304–1374) and Boccaccio (1313–1375). Petrarch was the first man we hear of who ever climbed a mountain just for the sake of climbing a mountain. This interest in nature as God made it is, as we have seen, good and proper. But Aquinas had opened the way to an autonomous Humanism, an autonomous philosophy, and once the movement gained momentum, there was soon a flood.

Nature versus grace

The vital principle to notice is that, as nature was made autonomous, nature began to 'eat up' grace. Through the Renaissance, from the time of Dante to Michelangelo, nature became gradually more totally autonomous. It was set free from God as the humanistic philosophers began to operate ever more freely. By the time the Renaissance reached its climax, nature had eaten up grace.

This can be demonstrated in various ways. We will begin with a miniature entitled *Grandes Heures de Rohan* painted about 1415. The story it portrays is a miracle story of the period. Mary and Joseph and the baby, fleeing into Egypt, pass by a field where a man is sowing seed, and a miracle happens. The grain grows up within an hour or so and is ready for harvesting. When the man goes to harvest it, pursuing soldiers come by and ask, 'How long ago did they pass by?' He replies that they passed when he was sowing the seed and so the soldiers turn back. However, it is not the story that interests us but rather the way in which the miniature is laid out. First of all, there is a great difference in the size of the figures of Mary and Joseph, the baby, a servant and the donkey which are at the top of the picture and which dominate it by their size, and the very small figures of the soldier and the man wielding the sickle at the bottom of the picture. Second, the message is made clear, not only by the size of the upper figures, but also by the fact that the background of the upper part of the miniature is covered with gold lines. Hence there is a total pictorial representation of nature and grace.

This is the older concept, with grace overwhelmingly important, and nature having little place.

In Northern Europe Van Eyck (1380–1441) was the one who opened the door for nature in a new way. He began to paint real nature. In 1410, a very important date in the history of art, he produced a tiny miniature. It measures only about five inches by three inches. But it is a painting with tremendous significance because it contains the first real landscape. It gave birth to every background that came later during the Renaissance. The theme is Jesus' baptism, but this takes up only a small section of the area. There is a river in the background, a very real castle, houses, hills and so on—this is a real landscape; nature has become important. After this, such landscapes spread rapidly from the north to the south of Europe.

Soon we have the next stage. In 1435, Van Eyck painted the *Madonna of the Chancellor Rolin*—now in the Louvre in Paris. The significant feature is that Chancellor Rolin, facing Mary, is the same size as she is. Mary is no longer remote, the Chancellor no longer a small figure, as would have been the case with the donors at an earlier period. Though he holds his hands in an attitude of prayer, he has become equal with Mary. From now on the pressure is on: how is this balance between nature and grace to be resolved?

Another man of importance, Masaccio (1401–1428), should be mentioned at this point. He makes the next big step in Italy after Giotto, who died in 1337, by introducing true perspective and true space. For the first time, light comes from the right direction. For example, in the marvellous Carmine Chapel in Florence, there is a window which he took into account as he painted his pictures on the walls, so that the shadows in the paintings fall properly in relation to the light from this window. Masaccio was painting true nature. He painted so that his pictures looked as though they were 'in the round'; they give a feeling of atmosphere; and he has introduced real composition. He lived only until he was twenty-seven, yet he opened almost the entire door to nature. With Masaccio's work, as with much of Van Eyck's, the emphasis on nature was such as could have led to painting with a true biblical viewpoint.

Coming on to Filippo Lippi (1406–1469), it is apparent that nature begins to 'eat up' grace in a more serious way than with Van Eyck's *Madonna of the Chancellor Rolin*. It was only a very few years before that artists would never have considered painting

Mary in a natural way at all—they would paint only a symbol of her. But when Filippo Lippi painted the Madonna in 1465 there is a startling change. He has depicted a very beautiful girl holding a baby in her arms, with a landscape that you cannot doubt was influenced by Van Eyck's work. This Madonna is no longer a far-off symbol; she is a pretty girl with a baby. But there is something more we need to know about this painting. The girl he painted as Mary was his mistress. And all Florence knew it was his mistress. Nobody would have dared to do this a few years before. Nature was killing grace.

In France, Fouquet (c. 1416–1480) painted, about 1450, the king's mistress, Agnes Sorel, as Mary. Everyone knowing the court who saw it knew that this was the king's current mistress. Fouquet painted her with one breast exposed. Whereas before it would have been Mary feeding the baby Jesus, now it is the king's mistress with one breast exposed—and grace is dead.

The point to be stressed is that, when nature is made autonomous, it is destructive. As soon as one allows an autonomous realm one finds that the lower element begins to eat up the higher. In what follows I shall be speaking of these two elements as the 'lower storey' and the 'upper storey'.

Leonardo da Vinci and Raphael

The next man to examine is Leonardo da Vinci. He brings a new factor into the flow of history, and comes closer to being a modern man than any before him. His dates (1452–1519) are important because they overlapped with the beginning of the Reformation. He is also very much a part of a significant shift in philosophic thinking. Cosimo the elder, of Florence, who died in 1464, was the first to see the importance of Platonic philosophy. Thomas Aquinas had introduced Aristotelian thinking. Cosimo began to champion Neo-platonism. Ficino (1433–1499), the great Neo-platonist, taught Lorenzo the Magnificent (1449–1492). By the time of Leonardo da Vinci, Neo-platonism was a dominant force in Florence. It became a dominant force for the simple reason that they needed to find some way to put something in the 'upper storey'. They introduced Neo-platonism in an attempt to reinstate ideas and ideals—that is, universals:

GRACE—UNIVERSALS

NATURE—PARTICULARS

A painting that illustrates this is *The School of Athens* by Raphael (1483–1520). In the room in the Vatican where this picture is located, on one wall a mural by Raphael represents the Roman Catholic Church, and this he balances with *The School of Athens*, representing classical pagan thought, on the opposite wall. In *The School of Athens* itself, Raphael portrays the difference between the Aristotelian element and the Platonic. The two men stand in the centre of the picture and Aristotle is spreading his hands downwards while Plato is pointing upwards.

This problem can be put in another way. Where do you find a unity when you set diversity free? Once the particulars are set free how do you hold them together? Leonardo grappled with this problem. He was

a Neo-platonist painter and, many people have said—
I think quite properly—the first modern mathe-
matician. He saw that if you begin with an autonomous rationality, what you come to is mathematics
(that which can be measured), and mathematics only
deals with particulars, not universals. Therefore you
never get beyond mechanics. For a man who realized
the need of a unity, he understood that this would not
do. So he tried to paint the soul. The soul is not the
Christian soul; the soul is the universal—the soul, for
example, of the sea or of the tree.[1] One of the reasons
he never painted very much was simply that he tried
to draw and draw in order to be able to paint the
universal. Needless to say, he never succeeded.

Giovanni Gentile, one of the greatest of Italian
philosophers until his fairly recent death, said that
Leonardo died in despondency because he would not
let go of the hope of a rational unity between the
particulars and the universal.[2] To have escaped this
despondency Leonardo would have had to have been a
different man. He would have had to let go his hope of
a unity above and below the line. Leonardo, not being
a modern man, never gave up the hope of a unified
field of knowledge. He would not, in other words,
give up the hope of educated man, who, in the past,
has been marked by this insistence on a unified field
of knowledge.

[1] SOUL—UNITY

MATHEMATICS—PARTICULARS—MECHANICS

[2] *Leonardo da Vinci* (Reynal & Co., New York, 1963), pp. 163–
174, Leonardo's Thought.

CHAPTER TWO

A unity of nature and grace

At this point it is important to note a historical relationship. Calvin was born in 1509. His *Institutes* were written in 1536. Leonardo died in 1519, the same year as the Leipzig Disputation between Luther (1483–1546) and Dr Eck. The king who took Leonardo to France at the close of his life was Francis I, the same king to whom Calvin addressed his *Institutes*. We come therefore to an overlapping of the Renaissance with the Reformation. To this problem of unity the Reformation gave an entirely opposite answer from that of the Renaissance. It repudiated both the Aristotelian and the Neo-platonic presentation. What was the Reformation answer? It said that the root of the trouble sprang from the old and growing Humanism in the Roman Catholic Church, and the incomplete Fall in Aquinas's theology which set loose an autonomous man. The Reformation accepted the biblical picture of a total Fall. The whole man had been made by God, but now the whole man is fallen, including his intellect and will. In contrast to Aquinas, only God was autonomous.

This was true in two areas. First of all there was

nothing autonomous in the area of final authority. For the Reformation, final and sufficient knowledge rested in the Bible—that is, Scripture Alone, in contrast to Scripture plus anything else parallel to the Scriptures, whether it be the church or a natural theology. Second, there was no idea of man being autonomous in the area of salvation. In the Roman Catholic position there was a divided work of salvation—Christ died for our salvation, but man had to merit the merit of Christ. Thus there was a humanistic element involved. The Reformers said that there is nothing man can do; no autonomous or humanistic, religious or moral effort of man can help. One is saved only on the basis of the finished work of Christ as He died in space and time in history, and the only way to be saved is to raise the empty hands of faith and, by God's grace, to accept God's free gift—Faith Alone.

So there is no division in either of these areas. There is no division in final normative knowledge—on the one hand, between what the church or natural theology would say and what the Bible would say; nor, on the other hand, between what the Bible and the rationalistic thinkers would say. Neither was there division in the work of salvation. It was Scripture Alone and Faith Alone.

Evangelical Christians need to notice, at this point, that the Reformation said 'Scripture Alone' and not 'the Revelation of God in Christ Alone'. If you do not have the view of the Scriptures that the Reformers had, you really have no content in the word 'Christ'—and this is the modern drift in theology. Modern theology uses the word without content because 'Christ' is cut away from the Scriptures. The Reformation followed the teaching of Christ Himself in linking the revelation Christ gave of God to the revelation of the written Scriptures.

The Scriptures give the key to two kinds of knowledge—the knowledge of God, and the knowledge of men and nature. The great Reformation confessions emphasize that God revealed His attributes to man in the Scriptures and that this revelation was meaningful to God as well as to man. There could have been no Reformation and no Reformation culture in Northern Europe without the realization that God had spoken to man in the Scriptures and that, therefore, we know something truly about God, because God has revealed it to man.

It is an important principle to remember, in the contemporary interest in communication and in language study, that the biblical presentation is that, though we do not have exhaustive truth, we have from the Bible what I term 'true truth'. In this way we know true truth about God, true truth about man and something truly about nature. Thus on the basis of the Scriptures, while we do not have exhaustive knowledge, we have true and unified knowledge.

The Reformation and man

We thus know something wonderful about man. Among other things, we know his origin and who he is—he is made in the image of God. Man is not only wonderful when he is 'born again' as a Christian, he is also wonderful as God made him in His image. Man has value because of who he was originally before the Fall.

I was recently lecturing in Santa Barbara, and was introduced to a boy who had been on drugs. He had a good-looking, sensitive face, long curly hair, sandals on his feet and was wearing blue jeans. He came to hear my lecture and said, 'This is brand new, I've never heard anything like this.' So he was brought along again the next afternoon, and I greeted him. He looked me in the eyes and said, 'Sir, that was a beautiful greeting. Why did you greet me like that?' I said, 'Because I know who you are—I know you are made in the image of God.' We then had a tremendous conversation. We cannot deal with people like human beings, we cannot deal with them on the high level of true humanity, unless we really know their origin—who they are. God tells man who he is. God tells us that He created man in His image. So man is something wonderful.

But God tells us something else about man—He tells us about the Fall. This introduces the other element which we need to know in order to understand man. Why is he so wonderful and yet so flawed? Who is man? Who am I? Why can man do these things that make man so unique, and yet why is man so horrible? Why is it?

The Bible says that you are wonderful because you are made in the image of God, but that you are flawed because, at a space-time point of history, man fell. The Reformation man knew that man was going to hell because of revolt against God. But the Reformation man and the people who, following the Reformation, built the culture of Northern Europe knew that, while man is morally guilty before the God who exists, he is not *nothing*. Modern man tends to think that he is nothing. These people knew that they were the very opposite of nothing because they knew that they were made in the image of God. Even though they were fallen, and, without the non-humanistic solution of Christ and His substitutionary death, would go to hell, this still did not mean that they were nothing. When the Word of God, the Bible, was listened to, the Reformation had tremendous results, both in people individually becoming Christians, and in general culture.

What the Reformation tells us, therefore, is that God has spoken in the Scriptures concerning both the 'upstairs' and the 'downstairs'. He spoke in a true revelation concerning Himself—heavenly things—and He spoke in a true revelation concerning nature—the cosmos and man. Therefore, they had a real unity of knowledge. They simply did not have the Renaissance problem of nature and grace! They had a real unity, not because they were clever, but because they had a unity on the basis of what God had revealed in both areas. In contrast to the Humanism which had been set free by Aquinas, and the Roman Catholic form of Humanism, there was, for the Reformation, no autonomous portion.

This did not mean that there was no freedom for art or science. It was quite the opposite; there was now possible true freedom within the revealed form. But, though art and science have freedom, they are not autonomous— the artist and the scientist are also under the revelation of the Scriptures. As we shall see, whenever art or science has tried to be autonomous, a certain principle has always manifested itself

—nature 'eats up' grace, and thus art and science themselves soon began to be meaningless.

The Reformation had some tremendous results, and made possible the culture which many of us love—even though our generation is now throwing it away. The Reformation confronts us with an Adam who was, using twentieth-century thought-forms, an unprogrammed man—he was not set up as a punch-card in a computer system. One thing that marks twentieth-century man is that he cannot visualize this, because modern man is infiltrated by a concept of determinism. But the biblical position is clear—man cannot be explained as totally determined and conditioned—a position that built the concept of the dignity of man. People today are trying to hang on to the dignity of man, and they do not know how to because they have lost the truth that man is made in the image of God. He was an unprogrammed man, a significant man in a significant history, and he could change history.

You have then, in Reformation thought, a man who is somebody. But you also have him in revolt: and he really revolts—it is not 'a piece of theatre'. And, because he is an unprogrammed man and really revolts, he has true moral guilt. Because of this, the Reformers understood something else. They had a biblical understanding of what Christ did. They understood that Jesus died on the cross in substitution and as a propitiation in order to save men from their true guilt. We need to learn that, when we begin to tamper with the scriptural concept of true, moral guilt, whether it be psychological tampering, theological tampering or any other kind of tampering, our view of what Jesus did will no longer be scriptural.

Christ died for a man who had true moral guilt because he had made a real and true choice.

More about man

We must now see something else about man. To do
this we must notice that everything in the biblical
system goes back to God. I love the biblical system as
a system. While we might not like the connotation of
the word *system*, because it sounds rather cold, this
does not mean that the biblical teaching is not a
system. Everything goes back to the beginning and
thus the system has a unique beauty and perfection
because everything is under the apex of the system.
Everything begins with the kind of God who is 'there'.
This is the beginning and apex of the whole, and
everything flows from this in a non-contradictory way.
The Bible says God is a living God and it tells us
much about Him, but, most significantly perhaps, for
twentieth-century man, it speaks of Him as both a
personal God and an infinite God. This is the kind of
God who is 'there', who exists. Furthermore, this is the
only system, the only religion, that has this kind of
God. The gods of the East are infinite by definition,
in the sense that they encompass all—the evil as well
as the good—but they are not personal. The gods of
the West were personal, but they were very limited.
The Teutonic, the Roman and the Greek gods were
all the same—personal but not infinite. The Christian
God, the God of the Bible, is personal-infinite.

This personal-infinite God of the Bible is the
Creator of all else. God created all things, and He
created them out of nothing. Therefore everything

else is finite, everything else is the creature. He alone is the infinite Creator. This can be set out as follows;

THE PERSONAL—INFINITE GOD

CHASM

MAN
ANIMAL
PLANT
MACHINE

He created man, the animals, the flowers and the machine. On the side of His infinity, man is as separated from God as is the machine. But, says the Bible, when you come on to the side of man's personality, you have something quite different. The chasm is at a different point:

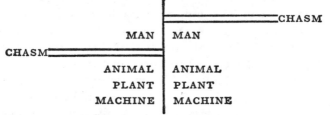

THE PERSONAL—INFINITE GOD

CHASM

MAN | MAN
CHASM
ANIMAL | ANIMAL
PLANT | PLANT
MACHINE | MACHINE

So man, being made in the image of God, was made to have a personal relationship with Him. Man's relationship is upward and not merely downward. If you are dealing with twentieth-century people, this becomes a very crucial difference. Modern man sees his relationship downward to the animal and to the machine. The Bible rejects this view of who man.is. On the side of personality you are related to God. You

26

are not infinite but finite; nevertheless, you are truly personal; you are created in the image of the personal God who exists.

Reformation, Renaissance and morals

There are many practical results of these differences between Renaissance and Reformation thought. Illustrations could come from a wide field. For example, the Renaissance set women free. So did the Reformation—but with a great difference. Jacob Burckhardt's work *The Civilization of the Renaissance in Italy*, published in Basel in 1860, is still a standard work on these subjects. He points out that the women of the Renaissance in Italy were free, but at the great cost of general immorality. Burckhardt (1818-1897) takes pages to illustrate this.

Why was it? It goes back to the then current view of nature and grace. These things are never merely theoretical, because men act the way they think:

LYRIC POETS—'SPIRITUAL LOVE'—IDEAL LOVE
NOVELISTS AND COMIC POETS—SENSUAL LOVE

In the upper section you have the lyric poets who taught 'spiritual love' and ideal love. Then, below, you have the novelists and the comic poets who taught sensual love. There was a flood of pornographic books. This element of the Renaissance period did not stop with the books themselves but carried over into the kind of lives men lived. The autonomous man found himself in a duality. You feel this in Dante, for example. He fell in love with one woman at first sight,

27

and he loved her all his life. Then he married another woman who bore his children and washed his dishes.

The simple fact is that this nature–grace division flowed over into the whole structure of Renaissance life, and the autonomous 'lower storey' always ate up the 'upper'.

The whole man

The Reformation's biblical view was, and is, very different. It is not a Platonic view. The soul is not more important than the body. God made the whole man and the whole man is important. The doctrine of the bodily resurrection of the dead is not an old-fashioned thing. It tells us that God loves the whole man and the whole man is important. The biblical teaching, therefore, opposes the Platonic, which makes the soul (the 'upper') very important and leaves the body (the 'lower') with little importance at all. The biblical view also opposes the humanist position where the body and autonomous mind of man become important, and grace becomes very unimportant.

The biblical position, stressed at the Reformation, says that neither the Platonic view nor the humanist view will do. First, God made the whole man and He is interested in the whole man. Second, when the historic space-time Fall took place, it affected the whole man. Third, on the basis of Christ's work as Saviour, and having the knowledge that we possess in the revelation of the Scriptures, there is redemption for the whole man. In the future, the whole man will be raised from the dead and will be redeemed perfectly. And Paul says in Romans 6 that even in the present life we are to have a substantial reality of the redemption of the whole man. This is to be on the basis of the shed blood of Christ and in the power of the Holy Spirit through faith, even though it will not be perfect in this life. There is the real lordship of Christ over the whole man. This is what the Reformers understood and what the Bible teaches. In Holland, for example, more than in Anglo-Saxon Christianity, they emphasized that this meant a lordship of Christ in culture.

So it means that Christ is equally Lord in both areas:

GRACE

NATURE

There is nothing autonomous—nothing apart from the lordship of Jesus Christ and the authority of the Scriptures. God made the whole man and is interested in the whole man, and the result is a unity. Thus at the same time as the birth of modern man in the Renaissance there was the Reformation's answer to his dilemma. In contrast, the dualism in Renaissance man has brought forth the modern forms of Humanism, with modern man's sorrows.

CHAPTER THREE

Early modern science

Science was very much involved in the situation that has been outlined. What we have to realize is that early modern science was started by those who lived in the consensus and setting of Christianity. A man like J. Robert Oppenheimer, for example, who was not a Christian, nevertheless understood this. He has said that Christianity was needed to give birth to modern science.[1] Christianity was necessary for the beginning of modern science for the simple reason that Christianity created a climate of thought which put men in a position to investigate the form of the universe.

Jean-Paul Sartre (b. 1905) states that the great philosophic question is that something exists rather than nothing exists. No matter what man thinks, he has to deal with the fact and the problem that there is something there. Christianity gives an explanation of why it is objectively there. In contrast to Eastern thinking, the Hebrew-Christian tradition affirms that God has created a true universe outside of Himself. When I use this term 'outside of Himself', I do not

[1] 'On Science and Culture', *Encounter*, October 1962.

mean it in a spatial sense; I mean that the universe is not an extension of the essence of God. It is not just a dream of God. There is something *there* to think about, to deal with and to investigate which has objective reality. Christianity gives a certainty of objective reality and of cause and effect, a certainty that is strong enough to build on. Thus the object, and history, and cause and effect really exist.

Further, many of the early scientists had the same general outlook as that of Francis Bacon (1561—1626), who said, in *Novum Organum Scientiarum*: 'Man by the Fall fell at the same time from his state of innocence and from his dominion over nature. Both of these losses, however, can even in this life be in some part repaired; the former by religion and faith, the latter by the arts and sciences.' Therefore science as science (and art as art) was understood to be, in the best sense, a religious activity. Notice in the quotation the fact that Francis Bacon did not see science as autonomous, for it was placed within the revelation of the Scriptures at the point of the Fall. Yet, within that 'form', science (and art) was free and of intrinsic value before both men and God.

The early scientists also shared the outlook of Christianity in believing that there is a reasonable God, who had created a reasonable universe, and thus man, by use of his reason, could find out the universe's form.

These tremendous contributions, which we take for granted, launched early modern science. It would be a very real question if the scientists of today, who function without these assurances and motivations, would, or could, have ever begun modern science.

Nature had to be freed from the Byzantine mentality and returned to a proper biblical emphasis; and it was the biblical mentality which gave birth to modern science.

Early science was natural science in that it dealt with natural things, but it was not naturalistic, for, though it held to the uniformity of natural causes, it did not conceive of God and man as caught in the machinery. They held the conviction, first, that God gave knowledge to men—knowledge concerning Himself and also concerning the universe and history; and, second, that God and man were not a part of the machinery and could affect the working of the machine of cause and effect. So there was not an autonomous situation in the 'lower storey'.

Science thus developed, a science which dealt with the real, natural world but which had not yet become naturalistic.

Kant and Rousseau

After the Renaissance-Reformation period the next crucial stage is reached at the time of Kant (1724–1804) and of Rousseau (1712–1778), although there were of course many others in the intervening period who could well be studied. By the time we come to Kant and Rousseau, the sense of the autonomous, which had derived from Aquinas, is fully developed. So we find now that the problem was formulated differently. This shift in the wording of the formulation shows, in itself, the development of the problem. Whereas men had previously spoken of nature and grace, by this time there was no idea of grace—the word did not fit any longer. Rationalism was now well developed and entrenched; and there was no concept of revelation in any area. Consequently the problem was now defined, not in terms of 'nature and grace', but of 'nature and freedom':

FREEDOM
———
NATURE

This is a titanic change, expressing a secularized situation. Nature has totally devoured grace, and what is left in its place 'upstairs' is the word 'freedom'.

Kant's system broke upon the rock of trying to find a way, any way, to bring the phenomenal world of nature into relationship with the noumenal world of universals. The line between the upper and lower storeys is now much thicker—and is soon to become thicker still.

At this time we find that nature is now really so totally autonomous that determinism begins to emerge. Previously determinism had almost always been confined to the area of physics, or, in other words, to the machine portion of the universe.

But, though a determinism was involved in the lower storey, there was still an intense longing after human freedom. However, now human freedom was seen as autonomous also. In the diagram, freedom and nature are both now autonomous. The individual's freedom is seen not only as freedom without the need of redemption, but as absolute freedom.

The fight to retain freedom is carried on by Rousseau to a high degree. He and those who follow him, in their literature and art, express a casting aside of civilization as that which is restraining man's freedom. It is the birth of the Bohemian ideal. They feel the pressure 'downstairs' of man as the machine. Naturalistic science becomes a very heavy weight— an enemy. Freedom is beginning to be lost. So men, who are not really modern men as yet and so have not accepted the fact that they are only machines, begin to hate science. They long for freedom even if the freedom makes no sense, and thus autonomous freedom and the autonomous machine stand facing each other.

What is autonomous freedom? It means a freedom in which the individual is the centre of the universe. Autonomous freedom is a freedom that is without restraint. Therefore, as man begins to feel the weight of the machine pressing upon him, Rousseau and others swear and curse, as it were, against the science which is threatening their human freedom. The freedom that they advocate is autonomous in that it has nothing to restrain it. It is freedom without limitations. It is freedom that no longer fits into the rational world. It merely hopes and tries to will that the finite individual man will be free—and all that is left is individual self-expression.

To appreciate the significance of this stage of the formation of modern man, we must remember that up until this time the schools of philosophy in the West, from the time of the Greeks onward, had three important principles in common.

The first is that they were rationalistic. By this is meant that man begins absolutely and totally from himself, gathers the information concerning the particulars, and formulates the universals. This is the proper use of the word rationalistic, and the way I am using it in this book.

Second, they all believed in the rational. This word has no relationship to the word 'rationalism'. They acted upon the basis that man's aspiration for the validity of reason was well founded. They thought in terms of antithesis. If a certain thing was true, the opposite was not true. In morals, if a thing was right, the opposite was wrong. This is something that goes as far back as you can go in man's thinking. There is no historic basis for the later Heidegger's position that the pre-Socratic Greeks, prior to Aristotle, thought differently. As a matter of fact it is the only way man can think. The sobering fact is that the only way one can reject thinking in terms of an antithesis and the rational is on the basis of the rational and the antithesis. When a man says that thinking in terms of an antithesis is wrong, what he is really doing is using the concept of antithesis to deny antithesis. That is the way God has made us and there is no other way to think. Therefore, the basis of classical logic is that A is not non-A. The understanding of what is involved in this methodology of antithesis, and what is involved in casting it away, is very important in understanding contemporary thought.

The third thing that men had always hoped for in philosophy was that they would be able to construct a unified field of knowledge. At the time of Kant, for example, men were tenaciously hanging on to this hope, despite the pressure against it. They hoped that by means of rationalism plus rationality they would find a complete answer—an answer that would encompass all of thought and all of life. With minor exceptions, this aspiration marked all philosophy up to and including the time of Kant.

Modern modern science

Before we move on to Hegel, who marks the next significant stage towards modern man, I want to take brief note of the shift in science that occurred along with this shift in philosophy that we have been discussing. This requires a moment's recapitulation. The early scientists believed in the uniformity of natural causes. What they did not believe in was the uniformity of natural causes *in a closed system*. That little phrase makes all the difference in the world. It makes the difference between natural science and a science that is rooted in naturalistic philosophy. It makes all the difference between what I would call modern science and what I would call modern modern science. It is important to notice that this is not a failing of science as science; rather that the uniformity of natural causes in a closed system has become the dominant philosophy among scientists.

Under the influence of the presupposition of the uniformity of natural causes in a closed system, the machine does not merely embrace the sphere of physics, it now encompasses everything. Earlier thinkers would have rejected this totally. Leonardo da Vinci understood the way things were going. We saw earlier that he understood that if you begin rationalistically with mathematics, all you have is particulars and therefore you are left with mechanics. Having understood this, he hung on to his pursuit of the universal. But, by the time to which we have now come in our study, the autonomous lower storey has eaten up the upstairs completely. The modern modern scientists insist on a total unity of the downstairs and the upstairs, and the upstairs disappears. Neither God nor freedom are there any more—everything is in the machine. In science the significant change came about therefore as a result of a shift in emphasis from the uniformity of natural causes to the uniformity of natural causes in a closed system.

One thing to note carefully about the men who have taken this direction—and we have now come to the present day—is that *these men* still insist on unity of knowledge. These men still follow the classical ideal of unity. But what is the result of their desire for a unified field? We find that they include in their naturalism no longer physics only; now psychology and social science are also in the machine. They say there must be unity and no division. But the only way unity can be achieved on this basis is by simply ruling out freedom. Thus we are left with a deterministic sea without a shore. The result of seeking for a unity on the basis of the uniformity of natural causes in a closed system is that freedom does not exist. In fact, love no longer exists; significance, in the old sense of man longing for significance, no longer exists. In other words, what has really happened is that the line has been removed and put up above everything—and in the old 'upstairs' nothing exists.

~~GOD~~	~~LOVE~~	M~~ORAL~~S
FR~~EED~~OM	SIGNI~~FIC~~ANCE	M~~AN~~

NATURE—PHYSICS, SOCIAL SCIENCES AND PSYCHOLOGY—DETERMINISM

Nature, having been made autonomous, has eaten up both grace and freedom. An autonomous lower storey will always eat up the upper. The lesson is: whenever you make such a dualism and begin to set up one autonomous section below, the result is that the lower eats up the upper. This has happened time after time in the last few hundred years. If you try artificially to keep the two areas separate and keep the autonomous in one area only, soon the autonomous will embrace the other.

Modern modern morality

This, of course, has repercussions in the sphere of morality. The twentieth-century pornographic writers all trace their origin to the Marquis de Sade (1740–1814). The twentieth century now treats him as a very important man—he is no longer just a dirty writer. Twenty or thirty years or so ago, if anyone was found with one of his books in England he was liable to have difficulties with the law. Today, he has become a great name in drama, in philosophy, in literature. All the 'black' (nihilistic) writers, the writers in revolt today, look back to de Sade. Why? Not only because he was a dirty writer, or even that he has taught them how to use sexual writing as a vehicle for philosophic ideas, but also because basically he was a chemical determinist. He understood the direction that things would have to take when man is included in the machinery. The conclusions he drew were these: if man is determined, then what *is* is right. If all of life is only mechanism—if that is all there is—then morals really do not count. Morals become only a word for a sociological framework. Morals become a means of manipulation by society in the midst of the machine. The word 'morals' by this time is only a semantic connotation word for non-morals. What is, is right.

This leads to the second step—man is stronger than woman. Nature has made him so. Therefore, the male has the right to do what he wishes to the female. The action for which they put de Sade in prison, both under the Monarchy and the Republic—taking a prostitute and beating her for his own pleasure—was by nature right. We get our word *sadism* from this. But it must not be forgotten that it is related to a philosophic concept. Sadism is not only pleasure in hurting somebody. It implies that what is, is right and what nature decrees in strength is totally right. Men like Sir Francis Crick today and even Freud, at his point of psychological determinism, are only saying what the Marquis de Sade has already told us—we are a part of the machine. But, if this is so, the Marquis de Sade's formula is inescapable—what is, is right. We are watching our culture put into effect the fact that, when you tell men long enough that they are machines, it soon begins to show in their actions. You see it in our whole culture—in the theatre of cruelty, in the violence in the streets, in the murders on the moors, in the death of man in art and life. These things, and many more like them, come quite naturally from the historical and philosophic flow which we are tracing.

What is wrong? Again, it goes back to Thomas Aquinas's insufficient view of the Fall which gives certain things an autonomous structure. When nature is made autonomous it soon ends up by devouring God, grace, freedom and eventually man. You can hang on to freedom for a while, desperately using the *word* freedom like Rousseau and his followers, but freedom becomes non-freedom.

Hegel

We come now to the next step of significance following Kant. We have said that there were three points that classical philosophy and thought had held on to —rationalism, rationality and the hope of a unified field of knowledge. Prior to Hegel (1770–1831), all philosophic pursuit had proceeded something like this: Someone had striven to construct a circle which would encompass all of thought and all of life. The next man said that this was not the answer but that he would provide one. The next man said, 'You have failed, but I will give you the answer.' The next man said, 'Not at all, this is it', and the next said, 'No!' It is hardly surprising that the study of the history of philosophy causes no great joy!

But by Kant's time the rationalistic rational possibilities are exhausted. Beginning with rationalistic presuppositions, the upper and lower 'storeys' are by his time in such great tension that they are ready to separate totally. Kant and Hegel are the doorway to modern man.

What did Hegel say? He argued that attempts had been made for thousands of years to find an answer on the basis of antithesis and they had not come to anything. Philosophic humanistic thought had tried to hang on to rationalism, rationality and a unified field, and it has not succeeded. Thus, he said, we must try a new suggestion. The long-term effect of this new approach of Hegel's has been that Christians today do not understand their children. It may sound strange, but it is true. What Hegel changed was something more profound than merely one philosophic answer for another. He changed the rules of the game in two areas: *epistemology*, the theory of knowledge and the limits and validity of knowledge: and *methodology*, the method by which we approach the question of truth and knowing.

What he said was this. Let us no longer think in terms of antithesis. Let us think rather in terms of thesis-antithesis, with the answer always being synthesis. In so doing he changed the world. The reason Christians do not understand their children is because their children do not think any longer in the same framework in which their parents think. It is not merely that they come out with different answers. The methodology has changed.

It is not because rationalistic man *wanted* to make this change. It was made out of desperation, because for hundreds of years rationalistic thought had failed. A choice was made, and the choice consisted in holding on to rationalism at the expense of rationality.

It is true that Hegel is usually classified as an idealist. He hoped for a synthesis which would have some relationship to reasonableness somehow. Nevertheless he opened the door to that which is characteristic of modern man. Truth as truth is gone, and synthesis (the both-and), with its relativism, reigns.

The basic position of man in rebellion against God is that man is at the centre of the universe, that he is autonomous—here lies his rebellion. Man will keep his rationalism and his rebellion, his insistence on total autonomy or partially autonomous areas, even if it means he must give up his rationality.

Kierkegaard and the Line of Despair

The man who follows Hegel, Kierkegaard (1813–1855), is the real modern man because he accepted what Leonardo and all other men had rejected. He put away the hope of a unified field of knowledge.

The formulation had been, first,

$$\frac{\text{GRACE}}{\text{NATURE}}$$

secondly,

$$\frac{\text{FREEDOM}}{\text{NATURE}}$$

It now became:

$$\frac{\text{FAITH}}{\text{RATIONALITY}}$$

In the following diagram, the line is a time line. The higher levels are earlier, the lower levels are later. The steps represent different disciplines.

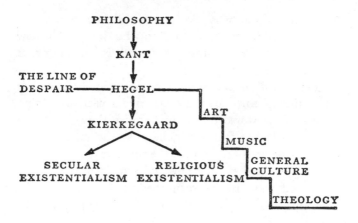

This new way of thinking spread in three different ways. In the first place it spread geographically, from Germany outward. Consequently Holland and Switzerland knew it before England, and America continued thinking in the old way much longer.

Second, it spread by classes. The intellectual was first affected. Then, through the mass media, it passed down to the workers. What it left was a middle-class that was not touched by it and often is still not touched by it. This middle-class group is, in many ways, a product of the Reformation; it is something to be thankful for as a source of stability. But now people in this group often do not understand the basis of its stability. They do not understand why they think in the old way—they are continuing to act out of habit and memory after they have forgotten why the old form was valid. Often they still think in the right way—to them truth is truth, right is right—but they

43

no longer know why. So how could they understand their twentieth-century children who think in the new way, who no longer think that truth is truth nor that right is right?

For the mass of people have received the new way of thinking through the mass media without analysing it. It is worse for them because they have been smashed in the face by it, because the cinema, television, the books they read, the press, magazines, have been infiltrated by the new thought-forms in an unanalysed way. In between the intellectuals and the working classes, you find a pocket—the upper-middle class. Undoubtedly, one of our difficulties is that most of our churches are in this upper-middle-class bracket, and the reason then why Christians are not understanding their own children is because the children are being educated into the other way of thinking. It is not merely that they think different things. They think differently. Their thinking has changed in such a way that when you say Christianity is true the sentence does not mean to them what it means to you.

The third way this has spread is by disciplines as shown in the preceding diagram: philosophy, then art, then music, then general culture, which could be divided into a number of areas. Theology comes last. In art, for example, you have the great impressionists, Van Gogh (1853–1890), Gauguin (1848–1903) and Cézanne (1839–1906). Then you have the post-impressionists. And here you come into the modern world. In music, Debussy (1862–1918) is the door. In general culture you can think of a man like the early T. S.

Eliot. The man who opened the door in theology is Karl Barth.[1]

I call this line in the diagram the Line of Despair. Not that everybody under the line cries, although some, like the painter Francis Bacon, do cry. Giacometti cried—he died crying.

What is this despair? It arises from the abandonment of the hope of a unified answer for knowledge and life. Modern man continues to hang on to his rationalism and his autonomous revolt even though to do so he has had to abandon any rational hope of a unified answer. Previously, educated men would not give up rationality and the hope of the unified field of knowledge. Modern man has given up his hope of unity and lives in despair—the despair of no longer thinking that what has always been the aspiration of men is at all possible.

[1] In *The God who is There* (Hodder and Stoughton, London, 1968) I have shown in detail the development under the Line of Despair in these areas (philosophy, art, music, general culture and theology), from the time when they went below the Line of Despair until the present.

CHAPTER FOUR

The leap

This step has brought us to Kierkegaard and the leap. With Kant we noticed that the line between nature and universals had widened considerably. What Kierkegaard's leap did was to put away the hope of any unity. After Kierkegaard we are left with this:

OPTIMISM MUST BE NON-RATIONAL

ALL RATIONALITY = PESSIMISM

The hope of a connecting link between the two spheres has disappeared. There is no permeation or interchange— there is a complete dichotomy between the upper and lower storeys. The line between the upper and lower storeys has become a concrete horizontal, ten thousand feet thick, with highly-charged barbed-wire fixed in the concrete.

What we are left with now runs something like this. Below the line there is rationality and logic. The upper storey becomes the non-logical and the non-rational. There is no relationship between them. In other words, in the lower storey, on the basis of all reason, man as man is dead. You have simply mathematics, particulars, mechanics. Man has no meaning, no purpose, no significance. There is only pessimism concerning man as man. But up above, on the basis of a non-rational, non-reasonable leap, there is a non-reasonable faith which gives optimism. This is modern man's total dichotomy.

The trouble with those of us who come out of a Christian background, or an upper-middle-class background, is that we cannot easily feel the thickness of this line in the way that it would be immediately understood by the twentieth-century man on the left bank in Paris—or at London University. We, coming out of our background, think there must be some interchange, but the answer of our age is, 'No, there never has been and there never will be.' When man thought there was an interchange it was just an illusion. On the basis of all reason, man is meaningless. He has always been dead as far as rationality and logic are concerned. It was a vain hope that man thought he was not dead.

This is what it means to say man is dead. It does not mean he was alive and died. He was always dead but did not know enough to know that he was dead.[1]

[1] In the Marxian state, the state was made the arbitrary absolute, putting forth detailed, arbitrary absolutes as laws, to give unity in the midst of their Hegelian materialism. The artists were at first the supporters of the Revolution, but then (with their modern art forms, based on modern thought-forms) they were a threat that had to be suppressed, because they challenged the sufficiency of the state and its laws in relationship to: 1. the meaning of the individual; 2. the attempt to restrain the natural development from Hegelian thinking towards increasing meaninglessness, as it has developed in the West. Theoreticians, like Adam Schaff of Warsaw, are now seeking a way to find a meaning for the individual without falling into the increasing chaos of the West. Hegelian relativism is now the consensus on both sides of the Iron Curtain;

From Kierkegaard there are two extensions—secular existentialism and religious existentialism.

Secular existentialism divides into three main streams: Jean-Paul Sartre (b. 1905) and Camus (1913–1960) in France, Jaspers (b. 1883) in Switzerland, Heidegger (b. 1889) in Germany. First, Jean-Paul Sartre. Rationally the universe is absurd, and you must try to authenticate yourself. How? By authenticating yourself by an act of the will. So if you are driving along the street and see someone in the pouring rain, you stop your car, pick him up and give him a lift. It is absurd. What does it matter? He is nothing, the situation is nothing, but you have authenticated yourself by an act of the will. But the difficulty is that authentication has no rational or logical content—all directions of an act of the will are equal. Therefore, similarly, if you are driving along and see the man in the rain, speed up your car and knock him down, you have in an equal measure authenticated your will. Do you understand? If you do, cry for modern man in such a hopeless situation.

Second, Jaspers. He is basically a psychologist, and speaks of a 'final experience': that is, an experience so

---

thus, in the most basic sense, the situation on both sides of the Iron Curtain is uniform, and on both sides man is dead. The West can point out the loss of the meaning of the individual through political suppression and brain-washing in the Communist states. But the individual is also losing meaning in the West: the question can be asked if this will not lead rapidly to the practical suppression of the individual in the West as well, in order to offset the growing chaos. One could think of John Kenneth Galbraith's suggestion of an 'academic, scientific establishment—State élite' or Allen Ginsberg's concept of an India-like caste system.

big that it gives you a certainty you are there and a hope of meaning—even though, rationally, you could not have such hope. The problem with this 'final experience' is that, because it is totally separated from the rational, there is no way to communicate its content either to someone else *or to yourself*. A student from the Free University in Amsterdam had been trying to hang on to such an experience. He had gone to *Green Pastures* one night and felt such an experience that he thought there must be some sense to life. I met him some two years after this had happened. He was close to suicide. Think about it—hanging on to some meaning to life only on the basis of such an experience, an experience which you cannot communicate even to yourself except on the basis of repeating that it had occurred. The morning after, it might be strong, but—two weeks later—two months—two years? How hopeless is hope based only on this final experience.

In addition, the final experience cannot be prepared for. Jaspers has therefore to tell his best students that they cannot be sure of having a final experience by committing suicide—for these people are serious enough to go out and do just that. There is no way to prepare for the final experience. The final experience is in the upper category—it just comes.

Third, you have what Heidegger called *Angst*. *Angst* is not just fear, for fear has an object. *Angst* is a vague feeling of dread—the uncomfortable feeling you have when you go into a house that might be haunted. Heidegger hung everything on this kind of basic anxiety. So the terms in which you express the upper storey make no difference at all. The basis of this system lies in the leap. Hope is separated from the rational 'downstairs'.

Today there are almost no philosophies in the classical sense of philosophy—there are anti-philosophies. Men no longer think they can get rational answers to the big questions. The Anglo-Saxon linguistic philosophers have shut themselves away from the great questions by limiting philosophy to a smaller area. They are concerned with the definition of words and have confined their operations to the lower storey. The existentialists have hung on more to a classical concept of philosophy in that they are dealing with the big questions, but they do this by accepting completely the dichotomy between rationality and hope.

What makes man a modern man is the existence of this dichotomy and not the manifold things he places, as a leap, in the upper storey. No matter what expression he places there, secular or religious, it still amounts to the same thing if it is rooted in this dichotomy. It is this that separates modern man from, on the one hand, Renaissance man, who had hope of a humanistic unity; and, on the other hand, from Reformation man, who actually possessed a rational unity above and below the line on the basis of the content of the biblical revelation.

Religious existentialism

The same general picture that emerges from secular existentialism is present in Karl Barth's system and the new theologies which have extended his system. There is no rational interchange above and below the line. He held, and holds, the higher critical theories, so the Bible contains mistakes, but we are to believe it anyway. 'Religious truth' is separated from the historical truth of the Scriptures. Thus there is no place for reason and there is no point of verification. This constitutes the leap in religious terms. Aquinas opened the door to an independent man downstairs, a natural theology and a philosophy which were both autonomous from the Scriptures. This has led, in secular thinking, to the necessity of finally placing all hope in a non-rational upstairs. Similarly, in neo-orthodox theology, man is left with the need to leap because, as the whole man, he cannot do anything in the area of the rational to search for God. Man, in neo-orthodox theology, is less than biblical fallen man. The Reformation and the Scriptures say that man cannot do anything to save himself, but he can, with his reason, search the Scriptures which touch not only 'religious truth' but also history and the cosmos. He not only is able to search the Scriptures as the whole man, including his reason, but he has the responsibility to do so.

The kind of words which are put in the upper storey do not change the basic system. As far as the system is concerned, the use of religious or secular terms makes no difference to it. What is particularly important to notice in this system is the constant appearance in one form or another of the Kierkegaardian emphasis on the necessity of the leap. Because the rational and logical are totally separated from the non-rational and the non-logical, the leap is total. Faith, whether expressed in secular or religious terms, becomes a leap without any verification because it is totally separated from the logical and the reasonable. We can now see, on this basis, how the new theologians can say that though the Bible, in the area of nature and history, is full of mistakes, this does not matter.

It does not matter what terms we adopt. The leap is common to every sphere of modern man's thought. Man is forced to the despair of such a leap because he cannot live merely as a machine. This, then, is modern man. It is modern man, whether expressed in his painting, his music, his novel, his drama or his religion.

The New Theology

In the New Theology the defined words are below the line:

NON-RATIONAL—CONNOTATION WORDS
_____
RATIONAL—DEFINED WORDS

Above the line the new theologian has undefined words. The 'leap theology' centres everything in the undefined word. Tillich, for example, speaks of the 'God behind God'—with the first word 'God' totally undefined. The defined words in the area of science and history are below the line; up above, there are only connotation words. Their value to him lies precisely in the fact that they *are* undefined.

The New Theology seems to have an advantage over secular existentialism because it uses words that have strong connotations as they are rooted in the memory of the race; words like 'resurrection', 'crucifixion', 'Christ', 'Jesus'. These words give an illusion of communication. The importance of these words to the new theologians lies in the illusion of communication, plus the highly motivated reaction men have on the basis of the connotation of the words. That is the advantage of the New Theology over secular existentialism and the modern secular mysticisms. One hears the word 'Jesus', one acts upon it, but it is never defined. The use of such words is always in the area of the irrational, the non-logical. Being separated from history and the cosmos, they are divorced from possible verification by reason downstairs, and there is no certainty that there is anything upstairs. We need to understand, therefore, that it is an act of desperation to make this separation, in which all hope is removed from the realm of rationality. It is a real act of despair, which is not changed merely by using religious words.

Upper storey experiences

Man made in the image of God cannot live as though he is nothing and thus he places in the upper storey all sorts of desperate things. In order to illustrate that it does not matter what one places in the upper storey, I shall try to show how manifold these things are. We have had examples of Sartre's 'existential experience', Jasper's 'final experience' and Heidegger's '*Angst*'. In each case man is dead, as far as rationality and logic are concerned.

Aldous Huxley made a titanic addition to this way of thinking. We find him using the term 'a first-order experience'. In order to have such a first-order experience he advocated the use of drugs. I have worked with many intelligent people taking LSD and have found hardly any of them who did not realize what they were doing was related to Aldous Huxley's teaching in regard to a 'first-order experience'. The point is that in the lower storey—nature—life makes no sense; it is meaningless. You take a drug in order to try to have a direct mystical experience that has no relation to the world of the rational. Jaspers, as we saw earlier, says you cannot prepare for this experience. Huxley, however, clung to the hope that you *can* prepare for it by taking drugs. So, as people are deciding that our culture is, in the words of Timothy Leary, a 'fake-prop-set society', they too are turning to drugs.

The basic reason that drugs are seriously taken today is not for escape or kicks but because man is desperate. On the basis of rationality and logic man has no meaning, and culture is becoming meaningless. Man is therefore trying to find an answer in 'first-order experiences'. This is what lies behind the modern drug mania. It is related to a thousand years of pantheism, for Eastern mystics have taken hashish for centuries to achieve religious experience. So it is nothing new, even though it is new to us. In *The Humanist Frame,*[1] in which Aldous Huxley wrote the last chapter, he was still, right before his death, pleading for the use of drugs by 'healthy people' for the 'first-order experience'. This was his hope.

Optimistic Evolutionary Humanism is yet another illustration of the fact that, once one accepts a dichotomy of the upper and lower storeys, what one then places in the upper storey makes no difference. Julian

[1] Allen and Unwin, London, 1961.

Huxley has propagated this idea. Optimistic Evolutionary Humanism has no rational foundation. Its hope is always rooted in the leap of *'mañana'*. In looking for proof one is always diverted to tomorrow. This optimism is a leap, and we are foolish in our universities to be intimidated into thinking that the humanists have a rational basis for the 'optimistic' part of their slogan. They have not—they are irrational. Julian Huxley himself has, in practice, accepted this for he has put down the basic proposition that men function better if they think that there is a god. There is no god, according to Huxley, but we will say there is a god. In other words, as Aldous Huxley is looking to drugs, so Julian Huxley is looking to a religious leap, even though to him it is a lie—that there is no god. This is why it is not out of line for Julian Huxley to write the introduction to Teilhard de Chardin's *Phenomenon of Man*.[1] They are both involved in the leap. The mere use of religious words in contrast to non-religious words changes nothing after the dichotomy and leap are accepted. Some positions seem further away from us and more shocking. Some seem closer—but there is no essential difference.

In a BBC Third Programme broadcast, Anthony Flew addressed himself to the question 'Must Morality Pay?'[2] He used the broadcast to show that, on the basis of his own presuppositions, morality does not pay. And yet he cannot stand this. At the very end he brings in out of thin air the concept that, in spite of the fact that morality does not pay, a man is

[1] Collins, London; Harper and Row, New York, 1959.
[2] *The Listener*, 13 October 1966.

not a fool to be scrupulous. This is a titanic leap without a basis as to why a man is not a fool to be scrupulous, nor any category as to what the word 'scrupulous' would mean.

The significant thing is that rationalistic, humanistic man began by saying that Christianity was not rational enough. Now he has come around in a wide circle and ended as a mystic—though a mystic of a special kind. He is a mystic with nobody there. The old mystics always said that there was somebody there, but the new mystic says that that does not matter, because faith is the important thing. It is faith in faith, whether expressed in secular or religious terms. The leap is the thing and not the terms in which the leap is expressed. The verbalization, *i.e.* the symbol systems, can change; whether the systems are religious or non-religious; whether they use one word or another is incidental. Modern man is committed to finding his answer upstairs, by a leap, away from rationality and away from reason.

Linguistic analysis and the leap

A short while ago I was leading a discussion in a particular British university where the linguistic philosophers are militant in their attack against the Christians. Some of them attended the discussion. As it went on it became obvious what they were doing. They were building their prestige in the area below the line in the reasonable definition of words. Suddenly, they leapt to an Optimistic Evolutionary Humanism above the line and attacked Christianity on the basis of the prestige which they had established in their own sphere. Some of them have quite properly established a reputation for rationality in the definition of words, but they then make a leap, changing their mask by attacking Christianity on the basis of a Humanism which has no relationship whatsoever to the downstairs area of linguistic analysis. As we have said, linguistic analysis is an anti-philosophy in the sense that these men have limited themselves in their concept of philosophy. They no longer ask the big questions classical philosophy has always asked. Therefore, anything they say in the area of these questions has no relationship to their discipline and the prestige it entails.

The interesting thing today is that as existentialism and, in a different way, 'defining philosophy' have become anti-philosophies, the real philosophic expressions have tended to pass over to those who do not occupy the chairs of philosophy—the novelist, the film producer, the jazz musician, the hippies and even the teenage gangs in their violence. These are the people who are asking and struggling with the big questions in our day.

CHAPTER FIVE

Art as the upper storey leap

We observed that from Rousseau's time the dichotomy was drawn between nature and freedom. Nature had come to represent determinism, the machine, with man in the hopeless situation of being caught in the machine. Then, in the upper storey, we find man struggling for freedom. The freedom that was being sought was an absolute freedom with no limitations. There is no God, nor even a universal, to limit him, so the individual seeks to express himself with total freedom, and yet, at the same time, he feels the damnation of being in the machine. This is the tension of modern man.

The field of art offers a variety of illustrations of this tension. Such tension affords a partial explanation of the intriguing fact that much of contemporary art, as a self-expression of what man is, is ugly. He does not know it, but he is expressing the nature of fallen man, which as created in the image of God is wonderful, yet now is fallen. As man strives to express his freedom in his autonomous fashion, much, though not all, of his art becomes meaningless and ugly. In contrast, much industrial design is becoming more orderly, with real beauty. I think the explanation for the growing beauty of some industrial design is that it has to follow the curve of what is there—it follows the form of the universe. This also illustrates how science as such is not autonomously free but must follow what is there. Even if the scientist or philosopher says that all is random and meaningless, once he moves out into the universe he is limited, no matter what his philosophic system is, for he must follow what he finds there. If science does not do this, it is not science but science fiction. Industrial design, like science, is also bound up with the form of the universe and therefore is often more beautiful than 'Art' (with a capital 'A'), which expresses man's rebellion, ugliness and despair. We now come to some of the various expressions of art as the upper storey leap.

Poetry: the later Heidegger

Heidegger could not accept his existentialism and changed his position—after he was seventy. In the book *What is Philosophy?*[1] he ends with the admonition 'but look at the poet'. When he says 'listen to the poet', he does not mean that we are to listen to the content of what the poet says. Content is immaterial —one might have six poets all contradicting each other. It does not matter because the content is in the area of rationality, the lower storey. What matters is that such a thing as poetry exists—and poetry is placed in the upper storey.

Heidegger's position is as follows. A part of Being is the being, man, who verbalizes. Consequently, be-

[1] Vision Press, London, 1958.

cause there are words in the universe, one has the hope of some kind of meaning to Being, *i.e.* what is. One just notes that the poet exists and, in his mere existence, the poet becomes the prophet. Because poetry is with us one hopes that there is more to life than merely what you know rationally and logically to be the case. Here then is another example of an irrational upstairs without any content.

Art: André Malraux

Malraux is an intriguing man. He came through existentialism, fought in the Resistance, took drugs, led a very rough and tumble life at times, and finally turned out to be the Minister of Culture of France. In his book *The Voices of Silence*[1] the last section is entitled 'Aftermath of the Absolute', and in it he shows that he understands very well the shift that has been caused by the modern death of a hope of an absolute.

There are a number of books at the present trying to come to terms with him. In the 6 October 1966 issue of *The New York Review of Books* several are dealt with. In this issue we find the following comment. 'All Malraux's works are torn . . . without help of resolution, between at least two positions: a basic anti-humanism (which is represented, depending on the circumstances, by intellectual pride, the will to power, eroticism and so on), and an ultimately irrational aspiration towards charity, or rationally unjustifiable choice in favour of man.'

In other words, there is a 'torn-ness' in Malraux—

[1] Secker and Warburg, London, 1954.

in the upper storey is placed something in art which has no rational basis whatsoever. It is the aspiration of a man separated from rationality. On the basis of rationality man has no hope, yet you look to art as art to provide it. It affords an integration point, a leap, a hope for freedom in the midst of what your mind knows is false. You are damned and you know it, and yet you look to art and try to find a hope that reasonably you know is not there. This review goes on to say, 'Malraux is rising above such despair by eloquently summoning himself and others to see the identity of man in the timelessness of art.' So Malraux's total work—his novels, his art history, his work as the French Minister of Culture—is a gigantic expression of this chasm and leap.

The system that surrounds us, of dichotomy and the leap, is a monolithic one. In England, Sir Herbert Read is in the same category. In *The Philosophy of Modern Art* [1] he shows he understands when he says about Gauguin: 'Gauguin substituted his love for beauty (as a painter) for man's love for his Creator.' But in his understanding he also says that reason must give place to the mystique of art—not only theoretically but as the starting place of education for tomorrow. [2] In Sir Herbert Read, art is again put forth as the answer achieved by the leap.

Picasso

Picasso furnishes another example. He had attempted to create a universal by means of abstraction. His

[1] Faber, London, 1952.
[2] 'Whatever Happened to the Great Simplicities', *Saturday Review*, 18 February 1967.

abstract paintings had gone so far that it was no longer a matter of distinguishing a blonde from a brunette, or a man from a woman, or even a man from a chair. Abstraction had gone to such an extent that he had made his own universe on the canvas—in fact he seemed at that time to be successfully playing at being god on his canvas. But at the moment when he painted a universal and not a particular, he ran head on into one of the dilemmas of modern man —the loss of communication. The person standing in front of the painting has lost communication with the painting—he does not know what the subject-matter is. What is the use of being god on a two-by-four surface when nobody knows what you are talking about!

However, it is instructive to see what happened when Picasso fell in love. He began writing across his canvas 'J'aime Eva'. Suddenly there was now a communication between the people looking at the picture and Picasso. But it was an irrational communication. It was communication on the basis that he loved Eva, which we could understand, but not on the subject-matter of the painting. Here again is the leap. On the basis of reason, as the painter tries rationally to make his own universal, communication is lost. But it is restored in a leap which is contrary to the rationality of his position. Yet because he is still a man he must leap, especially when he falls in love.

From that time on, it is possible to take Picasso's work and follow the curves of the paintings as he fell in and out of love. Later, for example, when he fell in love with Olga and married her, he painted her in a most human way. I am not saying the rest of his paintings are not great. He is a great painter, but he is a man lost. Picasso failed to do what he set out to do in his attempt to achieve a universal, and his whole life after this has been a series of tensions. When he fell out of love with Olga his paintings changed again. Then, a few years ago, I saw some of his work when he fell in love again, with Jacqueline. I said at the time, 'Picasso is in a new era—he loves this woman.' True enough he later married her—his second marriage. Thus, in his paintings of Olga and Jacqueline, in a manner contrary to almost all of his other work, he expresses the irrational leap in the symbol system of the form of his painting, but it is the same irrational leap which others express in words.

In passing, let us say that Salvador Dali did the same thing by painting connotation Christian art symbols when he took the leap from his old surrealism to his new mysticism. In his later work the Christian symbols are painted using their connotative effect, rather than verbalized, as in the New Theology. But this makes no difference. It is based on a leap, and an illusion of communication is given by using the connotative effect of the Christian symbols.

Bernstein

We are showing that we are faced with an almost monolithic concept today, of dichotomy and leap, and that once the leap is accepted, it really makes no difference what you place upstairs, or in what terms or even symbol systems the upstairs is expressed.

Leonard Bernstein, for example, in his *Kaddish*[1] indicated that music is the hope upstairs. The essence of modern man lies in his acceptance of a two-level situation, regardless of what words or symbols are used to express this. In the area of reason man is dead and his only hope is some form of a leap that is not open to consideration by reason. Between these two levels there is no point of contact.

Pornography

Modern pornographic writing is explicable in these terms too. There have always been such writings, but the new ones are different. They are not just dirty writings of the kind that were always available—many of today's pornographic works are philosophic statements. If one takes the works of somebody like Henry Miller, one finds that they are a statement that rationally and logically even sex is dead, yet in later writing he leaps into a pantheism for a hope of meaning.

Another element in modern pornographic writing comes out in the works of Terry Southern. He is the author of *Candy* and *The Magic Christian*. Despite the dirt and destructiveness he is making serious statements. Candy is called Candy Christian. This is significant. He is smashing the Christian position. But what does he put in its place? In the introduction to a book called *Writers in Revolt*[2] he takes the following line. He calls the introduction 'Towards the Ethics of a Golden Age', and proceeds to show how Western

[1] *Kaddish Symphony*, 1963 (Columbia KL6005 or KS6005).
[2] Berkeley Publishing Company, New York, 1963.

64

modern man is falling to pieces. He shows how modern man is only psychologically orientated. He has in particular one clever sentence in this statement of our culture's psychological orientation. 'Its implication, in terms of any previously operative philosophy or cultural structure prior to this century, is shattering, for its ultimate meaning is that there is no such thing as crime: it destroys the idea of crime.' He does not mean, of course, that we no longer have crime. He means that with psychological orientation 'crime' does not exist. No matter what it is, it is not seen as crime, nor as morally wrong.

Evangelical Christians tend to write off such people and then get into trouble over understanding modern man, for in reality these people are the philosophers of the day. Our university chairs of philosophy are in effect largely vacant. The philosophy is being written by the Southerns of this modern world. When you come to the end of this introduction I have quoted, you are left breathless at a terrific piece of writing. You feel like screaming and saying, 'Well, then, what is there?' The fantastic thing is that the end of the introduction says that they are writing pornographic material today in the hope that finally an ethic for the golden age will drop out. Thus pornographic writing is now put in the upper storey. They conceive of pornography as the ultimate release—it is the leap to freedom. They are smashing away at the downstairs deadness, and say that they will not have its tyranny. And although there is of course much trash as well, there is in these serious pornographic writings, struggling with this problem, the hope that pornography will provide a new golden age. This is

Rousseau and the autonomous freedom coming to a natural conclusion. Remember that in the Renaissance there was the dualistic separation like this:

LYRIC POETS—SPIRITUAL LOVE

NOVELISTS AND COMIC POETS (PORNOGRAPHIC)

But now rationalistic humanism has progressed logically to a total dichotomy between the upper and the lower, like this:

THE AUTONOMOUS PORNOGRAPHIC AS
THE ONLY HOPE OF FREEDOM AND OF MAN

RATIONALITY—MAN IS DEAD

This again is a mysticism with nobody there, a mysticism that flies in the face of rationality. There is nothing, and yet, driven by his aspirations—because he is made in the image of God—man tries all these overwhelming acts of desperation, even entertaining the hope that a golden age will drop out of Soho.

There has also been written recently a serious pornographic work in which, because there is no God, a woman puts herself into a man's hands to be beaten. The work states explicitly that, since no God exists, she wants to be possessed by someone, and thus in her alienation is glad of the beatings and pain as a proof of possession by *something, someone.*

These people are in total desperation. We are fighting for our lives. If we love men, this is no age for a lack of comprehension, no age to play small-sized games, and no age to fall into the same thought-form of duality without realizing it.

This note of desperation is reflected in the Theatre of the Absurd. The stress on the absurd recalls the whole structure of Sartre's thought. Man is a tragic joke in a context of total cosmic absurdity. He has been thrown up with aspirations which rationally have no fulfilment in the universe in which he lives. But this outlook as expressed in the Theatre of the Absurd goes beyond Sartre. Sartre says the universe is absurd but uses words and syntax as they are normally used. The Theatre of the Absurd, however, deliberately uses abnormal syntax and the devaluation of words to shout the more loudly that all is absurd.

Martin Esslin, well-known for his work in the BBC, has written a book on this subject which has a very interesting introduction, 'The Absurdity of the Absurd'.[1] He says that there are three steps in the Theatre of the Absurd. The first step is that you say to the bourgeois: Wake up! You have been asleep long enough. Wake him—kick his bed and pour a bucket of water over him through the absurd theatre. Then, as soon as he is awake, look him in the eye and tell him there is nothing there. That is the second step. But there is a third step, once again an upper-storey mysticism. This upper-storey mysticism is an attempt to communicate 'above' communication. As such, it is parallel to the Happenings and Environments following Marcel Duchamp, the battering of the senses by much electronic music, far-out cinema, the psychedelic elements in the latest Beatles records, and some elements in the theories of 'cool communication'

[1] *The Theatre of the Absurd* (Anchor Books, New York, 1961).

by Marshall McLuhan. This is not the place to deal with this subject in detail, but it is my conclusion that this communication, 'above' communication, with no continuity with the rational, cannot communicate content, but must be taken seriously as a vehicle of manipulation. However, we can see that of the three steps in the Theatre of the Absurd, two are towards pessimism while the third is again a mystical leap without any roots at all in the first two steps.

CHAPTER SIX

Madness

We still have not exhausted this subject of the leap. There are other areas where it shows itself. A recent book by Michel Foucault called *Madness and Civilization*[1] is important here. In a review of the book in *The New York Review of Books* (3 November 1966), entitled 'In Praise of Folly', the reviewer Stephen Marcus of Columbia University comments, 'What Foucault is finally against, however, is the authority of reason ... In this Foucault represents an important tendency in advanced contemporary thought. In his despair of the transcendent powers of rational intellect he embodies one abiding truth of our time—the failure of the nineteenth century to make good its promises.' In other words, the heirs of the Enlightenment had promised that they would provide a unified answer on the basis of the rational. Foucault maintains correctly that it has not fulfilled its promise. The reviewer continues: 'This is partly why he turns at the end to the mad and half-mad artists and thinkers of the modern age ... Through their utterances the world is arraigned; mediated by their madness, the

[1] Pantheon, New York, 1966.

language of their art dramatizes the culpability of the world and forces it to recognize itself and re-order its consciousness. One cannot, in good conscience, deny the force and truth of these observations; they catch a reality of the intellectual situation of the present moment—a moment that is coming to think of itself as post-everything, post-modern, post-history, post-sociology, post-psychology. . . . We are in the position of having rejected the nineteenth and twentieth century systems of thought, of having outworn them without having transcended them with new truth, or discovered anything of comparable magnitude to take their place.'

In other words, the rationalists have not found any kind of unity, or any other hope of a rational solution. So we find that Foucault follows Rousseau's thought to its conclusion: the ultimate in autonomous freedom is being crazy. It is a fine thing to be crazy, for then you are free.

THE NON-RATIONAL—THE REAL
FREEDOM IS MADNESS
_____

THE RATIONAL—MAN IS DEAD

It may be objected that this is a unique idea which Foucault and the reviewer have had, and it is therefore unimportant as totally extreme. And yet serious drug-taking is a self-imposed and, it is hoped, temporary mental illness. The results of drug-taking and schizophrenia are remarkably parallel, and this fact is understood by many drug-takers—and there are literally thousands taking drugs today. *Newsweek* (6 February 1967) tells of hippies in San Francisco using the tune of *We Shall Overcome* to the words, *We Are All Insane*. Foucault is not too far removed from Aldous Huxley. He is not to be thought of as too isolated to be of importance in understanding our day, and in understanding the end of duality and dichotomy. The logical end of the dichotomy, in which hope is separated from reason, is the giving up of all reason.

The 'upstairs' in film and television

This almost monolithic concept can be felt in the cinema and television as well as in the other areas to which we have already referred. The gifted cinema producers of today—Bergman, Fellini, Antonioni, Slesinger, the avant-garde cinema men in Paris, or the Double-Neos in Italy, all have basically the same message. People often ask which is better—American or BBC television. What do you want—to be entertained to death, or to be killed with wisely planted blows? That seems to be the alternative. BBC is better in the sense that it is more serious, but it is overwhelmingly on the side of the twentieth-century mentality. I happened to hear that programme on BBC television when the four-letter word was used. Such usage is obviously a serious departure from old standards, yet I would say if we were given a choice *and had to choose,* let us have ten thousand four-letter words rather than the almost subliminal presentation on English television of twentieth-century thinking without the four-letter words. The really dangerous thing is that our people are being taught this twentieth-century mentality without being able to understand what is happening to them. That is why this mentality has penetrated into the lower cultural levels as well as among the intellectuals.

Bergman said that all the first films he made were intended to teach existentialism. He then came to the view, like Heidegger before him, that this was not adequate. He therefore made a film—*The Silence*—which showed the radical change. *The Silence* is a statement of the belief that man is really dead. It introduced a new kind of cinema—the camera eye simply looks at life and reports it as meaningless in non-human terms. The film is a series of pictures with no human statement connected with them.

This outlook appears too in the 'Black' (nihilistic) writers of our day. This was also the importance of Capote's *In Cold Blood*. One of the things almost all the reviewers noticed concerning Capote's book is that there is no moral judgment made. It simply reports —he picked up the murder weapon and did this—the same kind of statement a computer, hooked up to a camera eye, would be able to make about it. Many people looked to *The Silence* and *In Cold Blood*, as well as to the works of other avant-garde writers, to open up a whole new area of cinema and literature. But what kind of cinema and literature is it? It has no judgments, no human elements, only statements that a camera or computer could make. Here is a vivid statement that the downstairs man is dead.

However, the most startling cinema statement today is not that man is dead downstairs, but the powerful expression of what man is above the line after the leap. The first of these films was *The Last Year at Marienbad*. This is not my guess. The film's director

72

explained that this is what he wanted the film to show. That is the reason for the long, endless corridors and the unrelatedness in the film. If below the line man is dead, above the line, after the non-rational leap, man is left without categories. There are no categories because categories are related to rationality and logic. There is therefore no truth and no non-truth in antithesis, no right and wrong—you are adrift.

Juliet of the Spirits is another of several pictures of this kind. A student in Manchester told me that he was going to see *Juliet of the Spirits* for the third time to try to work out what was real and what was fantasy in the film. I had not seen it then but I saw it later in a small art theatre in London. Had I seen it before I would have told him not to bother. One could go ten thousand times and never figure it out. It is deliberately made to prevent the viewer from distinguishing between objective reality and fantasy. There are no categories. One does not know what is real, or illusion, or psychological, or insanity.

Antonioni's *Blow-up* is the latest statement of the same message, the portrayal of modern man upstairs without categories. It underlines the vital point here: the fact that there are no categories is the reason that once the dichotomy is accepted, it is immaterial what one places upstairs.

Upper storey mysticism

The mysticism with nobody there, as we have termed it earlier, is therefore a mysticism without categories, so it does not matter upstairs whether you use religious or non-religious terms, art-symbol systems, or pornography.

The same principle characterizes the New Theology —not only is man dead below the line, but below the line God is dead also. The 'God is Dead' theologians say very clearly—'What is the use of talking about God in the upper storey when we do not know anything about him. Let us say quite honestly that God is dead.' With the background we have traced in general culture you can now see why these theologians are tired of the game. Why bother with all these godwords? Why not just say it is all over, we accept the rational conclusion of the downstairs that God is dead.

So current liberal theology can be set out like this:

NON-RATIONAL	JUST THE CONNOTATION WORD 'GOD' —NO CONTENT CONCERNING GOD— NO PERSONAL GOD
RATIONAL	GOD IS DEAD MAN IS DEAD

Upstairs, with the vacuum we have been talking about, they have no idea that there is anything that is in real and true correlation with the connotation borne along with the *word* god. All they have is a semantic answer on the basis of a connotation word. Up above, the New Theology is left with the philosophic other, the infinite, impersonal everything. This brings us in Western thought into proximity with the East. The new theologian has lost the unique infinite-personal God of biblical revelation and of the Reformation. Liberal theology of the current thinking has only god *words* as a substitute.

T. H. Huxley has proved to be a discerning prophet in all this. In 1890 [1] he made the statement that there would come a time when men would remove all content from faith and especially pre-Abrahamic scriptural narrative. Then: 'No longer in contact with fact of any kind, Faith stands now and forever proudly inaccessible to the attacks of the infidel.' Because modern theology has accepted the dichotomy and removed the things of religion from the world of the verifiable, modern theology is now in the position grandfather Huxley prophesied. Modern theology now differs little from the agnosticism or even the atheism of 1890.

So then, in our day, the sphere of faith is placed in the non-rational and non-logical as opposed to the rational and logical; the unverifiable as opposed to the verifiable. The new theologians use connotation words rather than defined words—words as symbols without any definition in contrast to scientific symbols that are carefully defined. Faith is unchallengeable because it could be anything—there is no way to discuss it in normal categories. Hundreds of years before, Aquinas had set up autonomous sections in his theological-philosophical system. The New Theology today is the result.

Jesus the undefined banner

The God is Dead school still uses the word Jesus. For example, Paul van Buren in *The Secular Meaning of the Gospel* says that the present-day problem is that

[1] *Science and Hebrew Tradition,* vol. 4 of *Huxley's Collected Essays* (Macmillan, London, 1902).

the *word* 'god' is dead. He goes on to point out, however, that we are no poorer by this loss, for all that
we need we have in the man Jesus Christ. But Jesus
here turns out to be a non-defined symbol. They use
the word because it is rooted in the memory of the
race. It is Humanism with a religious banner called
Jesus to which they can give any content they wish.
You find, therefore, that these men have made a
sudden transference and slipped the word Jesus as a
connotation word into the upper storey. So notice once
more that it does not matter what word you put up
there—even biblical words—if your system is centred
in the leap.

NON-RATIONAL   JESUS

RATIONALITY— GOD IS DEAD

 This emphasizes how careful the Christian needs to
be. In the *Weekend Telegraph* of 16 December 1966,
Marghanita Laski speaks of the new kinds of mysticisms which she sees developing and says, 'in any case
how could they be shown to be true or false?' The sum
of her point is that men are removing religious things
out of the world of the discussable and putting them
into the non-discussable, where you can say anything
without fear of proof or disproof.
 The evangelical Christian needs to be careful because some evangelicals have recently been asserting
that what matters is not setting out to prove or dis-
prove propositions; what matters is an encounter with
Jesus. When a Christian has made such a statement he
has, in an analysed or unanalysed form, moved upstairs.

RATIONAL—ONE DOES NOT SET ABOUT PROVING
OR DISPROVING PROPOSITIONS

If we think that we are escaping some of the pressures of the modern debate by playing down propositional Scripture and simply putting the word 'Jesus' or 'experience' upstairs, we must face this question: What difference is there between doing this and doing what the secular world has done in its semantic mysticism, or what the New Theology has done? At the very least the door has been opened for man to think it is the same thing. Certainly men in the next generation will tend to make it the same thing.

If what is placed upstairs is separated from rationality, if the Scriptures are not discussed as open to verification where they touch the cosmos and history, why should one then accept the evangelical upstairs any more than the upstairs of the modern radical theology? On what basis is the choice to be made? Why should it not just as well be an encounter under the name Vishnu? Indeed, why should one not seek an experience, without the use of any such words, in a drug experience?

Our urgent need today is to understand the modern system as a whole, and to appreciate the significance of duality, dichotomy and the leap. The upstairs, we have seen, can take many forms—some religious, some secular, some dirty, some clean. The very essence of the system leads to the fact that the type of words used upstairs does not matter—even such a well-loved word as 'Jesus'.

I have come to the point where, when I hear the word 'Jesus'—which means so much to me because of the Person of the historic Jesus and His work—I listen carefully because I have with sorrow become more afraid of the word 'Jesus' than almost any other word in the modern world. The word is used as a contentless banner, and our generation is invited to follow it. But there is no rational, scriptural content by which to test it, and thus the word is being used to teach the very opposite things from those which Jesus taught. Men are called to follow the word with highly motivated fervency, and nowhere more than in the new morality which follows the New Theology. It is now Jesus-like to sleep with a girl or a man, if she or he needs you. As long as you are trying to be human you are being Jesus-like to sleep with the other person, at the cost, be it noted, of breaking the specific morality which Jesus taught. But to these men this does not matter, because that is downstairs in the area of rational scriptural content.

We have come then to this fearsome place where the word 'Jesus' has become the enemy of the Person Jesus, and the enemy of what Jesus taught. We must fear this contentless banner of the word 'Jesus' not because we do not love Jesus, but because we do love Him. We must fight this contentless banner, with its deep motivations, rooted into the memories of the race, which is being used for the purpose of sociological form and control. We must teach our spiritual children to do the same.

This accelerating trend makes me wonder whether, when Jesus said that towards the end-time there will be other Jesuses, He meant something like this. We must never forget that the great enemy who is coming is the anti-Christ. He is not anti-non-Christ. He is anti-Christ. Increasingly over the last few years the word 'Jesus', separated from the content of the Scriptures, has become the enemy of the Jesus of history, the Jesus who died and rose and who is coming again and who is the eternal Son of God. So let us take care. If evangelical Christians begin to slip into a dichotomy, to separate an encounter with Jesus from the content of the Scriptures (including the discussable and the verifiable), we shall, without intending to, be throwing ourselves and the next generation into the millstream of the modern system. This system surrounds us as an almost monolithic consensus.

CHAPTER SEVEN

Rationality and faith

Some of the consequences of pitting faith against rationality in an unbiblical manner are as follows.

The first consequence of putting Christianity in an upper storey concerns morality. The question arises as to how we can establish a relationship from an upstairs Christianity down into the area of morals in daily life. The simple answer is that you cannot. As we have seen, there are no categories upstairs, and so there is no way for the upstairs to provide categories! Consequently what really forms the 'Christlike' act today is simply what the consensus of the church or the consensus of society makes up its mind is desirable at that particular moment. You cannot have real morals in the real world after you have made this separation. What you have is merely a relative set of morals.

The second consequence of this separation is that you have no adequate basis for law. The whole Reformation system of law was built on the fact that God had revealed something real down into the common things of life. There is a beautiful painting by Paul Robert in Switzerland's old Supreme Court

Building in Lausanne. It is called *Justice Instructing the Judges*. Down in the foreground of the large mural is shown much litigation—the wife against the husband, the architect against the builder, and so on. How are the judges going to judge between them? This is the way we judge in a Reformation country, says Paul Robert. He has portrayed Justice pointing with her sword to a book upon which are the words 'The Law of God'. For Reformation man there was a basis for law. Modern man has not only thrown away Christian theology, he has thrown away the possibility of what our forefathers had as a basis for morality and law.

Another consequence is that this throws away the answer to the problem of evil. Christianity's answer rests in the historic, space-time, real and complete Fall. Aquinas's error was an incomplete Fall. But the true Christian position is that, in space and time and history, there was an unprogrammed man who made a choice, and actually rebelled against God. Once you remove this you have to face Baudelaire's profound statement, 'If there is a God, He is the devil', or Archibald MacLeish's statement in his play *J.B.*, 'If he is God he cannot be good, if he is good he cannot be God'. Without Christianity's answer that God made a significant man in a significant history with evil being the result of Satan's and then man's historic space-time revolt, there is no answer but to accept Baudelaire's statement with tears. Once the historic Christian answer is put away, all we can do is to leap upstairs and say that against all reason God is good. Notice that if we accept a duality, thinking that we thus escape conflict with modern culture and the consensus of thinking, we are trapped in an illusion, for when we move on a few steps we will find that we come out at the same place where they are.

The fourth consequence of placing Christianity in the upper storey is that we thus throw away our chance of evangelizing real twentieth-century people in the midst of their predicament. Modern man longs for a different answer than the answer of his damnation. He did not accept the Line of Despair and the dichotomy because he wanted to. He accepted it because, on the basis of the natural development of his rationalistic presuppositions, he had to. He may talk bravely at times, but in the end it *is* despair.

Christianity has the opportunity, therefore, to speak clearly of the fact that its answer has the very thing that modern man has despaired of — the unity of thought. It provides a unified answer for the whole of life. It is true that man will have to renounce his rationalism, but then, on the basis of what can be discussed, he has the possibility of recovering his rationality. You may now see why I stressed so strongly, earlier, the difference between rationalism and rationality. Modern man has lost the latter. But he can have it again with a unified answer to life on the basis of what is open to verification and discussion.

Let Christians remember, then, that if we fall into the trap against which I have been warning, what we have done, amongst other things, is to put ourselves in the position where in reality we are only saying with evangelical words what the unbeliever is saying with his words. In order to confront modern man truly you must not have the dichotomy. You must have the Scriptures speaking true truth both about

God Himself and about the area where the Bible touches history and the cosmos. This is what our forefathers in the Reformation grasped so well.

On the side of infinity, as we saw before, we are separated from God entirely, but on the side of personality we are made in the image of God. So God can speak and tell us about Himself—not exhaustively, but truly. (We could not, after all, know anything exhaustively as finite creatures.) Then He has told us about things in the finite created realm, too. He has told us true things about the cosmos and history. Thus, we are not adrift.

But you cannot have this answer unless you hold to the Reformation view of the Scriptures. It is not a question of God revealing Himself in Jesus Christ only, because there is not enough content in this if it is separated from the Scriptures. It then becomes only another contentless banner, for all we know of what that revelation of Christ was comes from the Scriptures. Jesus Himself did not make a distinction between His authority and the authority of the written Scriptures. He acted upon the unity of His authority and the content of the Scriptures.

There is the personal element involved in all this. Christ is Lord of all—over every aspect of life. It is no use saying He is the Alpha and Omega, the beginning and the end, the Lord of all things, if He is not the Lord of my whole unified intellectual life. I am false or confused if I sing about Christ's lordship and contrive to retain areas of my own life that are autonomous. This is true if it is my sexual life that is autonomous, but it is at least equally true if it is my intellectual life that is autonomous—or even my intellectual life in a highly selective area. Any autonomy is wrong. Autonomous science or autonomous art is wrong, if by autonomous science or art we mean it is free from the content of what God has told us. This does not mean that we have a static science or art—just the opposite. It gives us the form inside which, being finite, freedom is possible. Science and art cannot be placed in the framework of an autonomous downstairs without coming to the same tragic end that has occurred throughout history. We have seen that in every case in which the downstairs was made autonomous, no matter what name it was given, it was not long before the downstairs ate up the upstairs. Not only God disappeared but freedom and man as well.

The Bible can stand on its own

Often people say to me, 'How is it that you seem to be able to communicate with these far-out people? You seem to be able to talk in such a way that they understand what you're saying, even if they do not accept it'. There may be a number of reasons why this is so, but one is that I try to get them to consider the biblical system and its truth without an appeal to blind authority—that is, as though believing meant believing just because one's family did, or as though the intellect had no part in the matter.

This is the way I became a Christian. I had gone to a 'liberal' church for many years. I decided that the only answer, on the basis of what I was hearing, was agnosticism or atheism. On the basis of liberal theology I do not think I have ever made a more logical decision in my life. I became an agnostic, and then I began to read the Bible for the first time—in order to place it against some Greek philosophy I was reading. I did this as an act of honesty in so far as I had given up what I thought was Christianity but had never read the Bible through. Over a period of about six months I became a Christian because I was convinced that the full answer which the Bible presented was alone sufficient to the problems I then knew, and sufficient in a very exciting way.

I have always tended to think visually, so I thought of my problems as balloons floating in the sky. I did not know then as many of the basic problems of men's thought as I know now. But what was exciting to me (and *is* exciting) was that, when I came to the Bible, I found it did not shoot down the problems, as an anti-aircraft gun would, knocking down the individual balloons, but something far more exciting. It answered the problems in the sense that I, limited though I was, could stand as though having a cable in my hand with all the problems linked together as a system, in the framework of what the Bible says truth is. Over and over again I have found my personal experience repeated. It is possible to take the system the Bible teaches, put it down in the market place of the ideas of men and let it stand there and speak for itself.

Let us notice that the system of the Bible is excitingly different from any other, because it is the only system in religion or philosophy that tells us why a person may do what every man must do, that is, begin with himself. There is, in fact, no other way to begin apart from ourselves—each man sees through his own eyes—and yet this involves a real problem. What right have I to begin here? No other system explains my right to do so. But the Bible gives me an answer as to why I can do what I must do, that is to begin with myself.

The Bible says, first of all, that in the beginning all things were created by a personal-infinite God, who had always existed. So what is, therefore, is intrinsically personal rather than impersonal. Then the Bible says that He created all things outside of Himself. The term 'outside of Himself' is, I think, the best way to express creation to twentieth-century people. We do not mean to use the phrase in a spatial sense, but to deny that creation is any kind of pantheistic extension of God's essence. God exists—a personal God who has always existed—and He has created all other things outside of Himself. Thus, because the universe begins with a truly personal beginning, love and communication (which are a burden of twentieth-century men's hearts) are not contrary to that which intrinsically is. The universe began in a personal as against an impersonal beginning, and, as such, those longings of love and communication which man has are not contrary to that which intrinsically is. And the world is a real world, because God has created it truly outside of Himself. What He has created is objectively real, thus there is true historic cause and effect. There is a true history and there is a true me.

In this setting of a significant history, the Bible says that God made man in a special way, in His own image. If I do not understand that man's basic relationship is upward, I must try to find it downward. In relating it downward, a person is very old-fashioned today if he finally relates himself to the animals. Today, modern man seeks to relate himself to the machine.

But the Bible says that my line of reference need not lead downward. It is upward because I have been made in God's image. Man is not a machine.

If the intrinsically personal origin of the universe is rejected, what alternative outlook can anyone have? It must be said emphatically that there is no final answer except that man is a product of the impersonal, plus time, plus chance. No-one has ever succeeded in finding personality on this basis, though many, like the late Teilhard de Chardin, have tried. It cannot be done. The conclusion that we are the natural products of the impersonal, plus time and chance, is the only one, unless we begin with personality. And no-one has shown how time plus chance can produce a qualitative change from impersonal to personal.

If this were true, we would be hopelessly caught. But, when the Bible says that man is created in the image of a personal God, it gives us a starting-point. No humanistic system has provided a justification for man to begin with himself. The Bible's answer is totally unique. At one and the same time it provides the reason why a man may do what he must do, start with himself; and it tells him the adequate reference point, the infinite-personal God. This is in complete contrast to other systems in which man begins with himself, neither knowing why he has a right to begin from himself, nor in what direction to begin inching along.

When we talk about the possibility of men beginning from themselves to understand the meaning of life and the universe, we must be careful to define clearly what we mean. There are two concepts or ideas of knowing which must be kept separate. The first is the rationalistic or humanistic concept, namely that man, beginning totally independent and autonomous of all else, can build a bridge towards ultimate truth—as if attempting to build a cantilever bridge out from himself across an infinite gorge. This is not possible, because man is finite and, as such, he has nothing toward which he can point with certainty. He has no way, beginning from himself, to set up sufficient universals. Sartre has seen this very clearly when, as a result of finding no infinite reference point, he comes to the conclusion that everything must be absurd.

The second concept is the Christian one. That is, as man has been created in God's image, he can begin with himself—not as infinite but as personal; plus the important fact (as we shall see below) that God has given to fallen man content-ful knowledge which he desperately needs.

The fact that man has fallen does not mean that he has ceased to bear God's image. He has not ceased to be man because he is fallen. He can love, though he is fallen. It would be a mistake to say that only a Christian can love. Moreover, a non-Christian painter can still paint beauty. And it is because they can still do these things that they manifest that they are God's image-bearers or, to put it another way, they assert their unique 'mannishness' as men.

So it is a truly wonderful thing that, although man is twisted and corrupted and lost as a result of the Fall, yet he is still man. He has become neither a machine nor an animal nor a plant. The marks of mannishness are still upon him—love, rationality, longing for significance, fear of non-being, and so on. This is the case even when his non-Christian system leads him to say these things do not exist. It is these things which distinguish him from the animal and plant world and from the machine. On the other hand, beginning only from himself autonomously, it is quite obvious that, being finite, he can never reach any absolute answer. This would be true if only on the basis of the fact that he is finite; but to this must be added, since the Fall, the fact of his rebellion. He rebels against, and perverts, the testimony of what exists—the external universe and its form, and the mannishness of man.

The source of the knowledge we need

In this setting the Bible sets forth its own statement of what the Bible itself is. It presents itself as God's communication of propositional truth, written in verbalized form, to those who are made in God's image. Functioning on the presupposition of the uniformity of natural causes in a closed system, both the secular and the unbiblical theological thinking of today would say that this is impossible. But that is precisely what the Bible says it sets forth. We may take, for example, what occurred at Sinai.[1] Moses says to the people, 'You saw; you heard.' What they heard (along with other

[1] Deuteronomy 5: 23, 24.

things) was a verbalized propositional communication from God to man, in a definite, historic space-time situation. It was not some kind of contentless, existential experience, nor an anti-intellectual leap. We find exactly the same kind of communication occurring in the New Testament, as for example when Christ spoke to Paul in Hebrew on the Damascus road. Therefore, on one hand we have the kind of propositional communication God gives in the Scriptures. On the other hand we see to whom this propositional communication is directed.

The Bible teaches that, though man is hopelessly lost, he is not nothing. Man is lost because he is separated from God, his true reference point, by true moral guilt. But he never will be nothing. Therein lies the horror of his lostness. For man to be lost, in all his uniqueness and wonder, is tragic.

We must not belittle man's achievements—in science, for instance, man's achievements demonstrate that he is not junk, though the ends to which he often puts them show how lost he is. Our forefathers, though they believed man was lost, had no problem concerning man's significance. Man can influence history, including his own eternity and that of others. This view sees man, as man, as something wonderful.

In contrast to this there is the rationalist who has determinedly put himself at the centre of the universe and insists on beginning autonomously with only the knowledge he can gather, and has ended up finding himself quite meaningless. It comes to the same thing as Zen Buddhism, which expresses so accurately the view of modern man: 'Man enters the water and causes no ripple.' The Bible says he causes ripples that *never* end. As a sinner, man cannot be selective in his significance, so he leaves behind bad as well as good marks in history, but certainly he is not a zero.

Christianity is a system which is composed of a set of ideas which can be discussed. By 'system' we do not mean a scholastic abstraction, nevertheless we do not shrink from using this word. The Bible does not set out unrelated thoughts. The system it sets forth has a beginning and moves from that beginning in a non-contradictory way. The beginning is the existence of the infinite-personal God as Creator of all else. Christianity is not just a vague set of incommunicable experiences, based on a totally unverifiable 'leap in the dark'. Neither conversion (the beginning of the Christian life) nor spirituality (the growth) should be such a leap. Both are firmly related to the God who is there and the knowledge He has given us—and both involve the whole man.

The 'leap in the dark' mentality

Modern man has come to his position because he has accepted a new attitude in regard to truth. Nowhere is this more clearly and yet tragically seen than in modern theology.

In order to see this new attitude to truth in perspective, let us consider two other concepts of truth: first that of the Greeks and then that of the Jews. Often the Greek concept of truth was a nicely balanced metaphysical system brought into harmony with itself at all points. The Jewish and biblical concept of truth is different. It is not that the rational concept which the Greeks held to was unimportant to the Jews, for both the Old and the New Testaments function on the basis of that which can be reasonably discussed; but, to the Jewish mind, something firmer was needed. And the firmer base was an appeal to real history—history in space and in time which could be written down and discussed as history.

The modern view of truth drives a wedge between the Greek and Jewish views, but it does so at the wrong point. Those who hold the modern view would picture the Greeks as holding to rational truth and the Jews as being existentialists. In this way they would seek to claim the Bible for themselves. This is ingenious, but a complete mistake. The Jewish concept is separated from the Greek in that the Jewish was rooted in space-time history and not just a balanced system. But the Jewish and biblical concept of truth is much closer to the Greek than to the modern, in the sense that it does not deny that which is a part of the mannishness of man—the longing for rationality, that which can be reasonably thought about and discussed in terms of antithesis.

The unchanging in a changing world

There are two things we need to grasp firmly as we seek to communicate the gospel today, whether we are speaking to ourselves, to other Christians or to those totally outside.

The first is that there are certain unchangeable facts which are true. These have no relationship to the shifting tides. They make the Christian system what it is, and if they are altered, Christianity becomes something else. This must be emphasized because there are evangelical Christians today who, in all sincerity, are concerned with their lack of communication, but in order to bridge the gap they are tending to change what must remain unchangeable. If we do this we are no longer communicating Christianity, and what we have left is no different from the surrounding consensus.

But we cannot present a balanced picture if we stop here. We must realize that we are facing a rapidly changing historical situation, and if we are going to talk to people about the gospel we need to know what is the present ebb and flow of thought-forms. Unless we do this the unchangeable principles of Christianity will fall on deaf ears. And if we are going to reach the intellectuals and the workers, both groups right outside our middle-class churches, then we shall need to do a great deal of heart-searching as to how we may speak what is eternal into a changing historical situation.

It is much more comfortable, of course, to go on speaking the gospel only in familiar phrases to the middle classes. But that would be as wrong as if, for example, Hudson Taylor had sent missionaries to China and then told them to learn only one of three separate dialects that the people spoke. In such a case, only one group out of three *could* hear the gospel. We cannot imagine Hudson Taylor being so hard-hearted. Of course he knew that men do not believe without a work of the Holy Spirit in their hearts, and his life was a life of prayer for this to happen, but he also knew that men cannot believe without hearing the gospel. Each generation of the church in each setting has the responsibility of communicating the gospel in understandable terms, considering the language and thought-forms of that setting.

In a parallel way we are being as overwhelmingly unfair, even selfish, towards our own generation, as if the missionaries had deliberately spoken in only one dialect. The reason we often cannot speak to our children, let alone other people's, is because we have never taken time to understand how different their thought-forms are from ours. Through reading and education and the whole modern cultural bombardment of mass media, even today's middle-class children are becoming thoroughly twentieth-century in outlook. In crucial areas many Christian parents, ministers and teachers are as out of touch with many of the children of the church, and the majority of those outside, as though they were speaking a foreign language.

So what is said in this book is not merely a matter of intellectual debate. It is not of interest only to academics. It is utterly crucial for those of us who are serious about communicating the Christian gospel in the twentieth century.

INDEX